NATIONAL GEOGRAPHIC KiDS

# LITTLE KIDS FIRST Nature Guide

# EXPLORE THE BEACH

**Alli Brydon**

NATIONAL GEOGRAPHIC
WASHINGTON, D.C.

COMMON DOLPHIN

# Table of CONTENTS

CONCH SHELL

GREEN TURTLE

MOON JELLY

SARGASSUM

HARBOR SEAL

# Beautiful Beaches

A beach is an area of land that touches the water. The land can be made of sand, pebbles, rocks, shells, and more. Beaches are found along lakes, rivers, and oceans. This book explores ocean beaches.

There are so many **things to discover** at the beach!

BEACHES ARE ALSO CALLED **SEASHORES OR COASTS.**

HERMIT CRAB

DUNE GRASS

PUFFIN

LIMPET SHELLS

CONCH SHELL

SEA STAR

# Let's Explore!

To explore at the beach, use your senses. Use your eyes to look up, down, and all around. Use your ears to listen to birds squawking and water splashing. Use your toes to feel scratchy sand and cool water.
Use your nose to sniff the salty air!

When you spot an animal or plant, notice its shape, color, and size. When you pick up shells and rocks, take a close look. Are they small or large? What shape are they? Are they smooth or bumpy?

**WHAT WOULD YOU LIKE TO FIND AT THE BEACH?**

If you find a **word you don't know,** look it up in the **glossary on page 46.**

## STAY SAFE!

Always have a grown-up with you at the beach. Do not go in the water alone. Leave any animals you find where they are. The beach is their home.

# WHAT TO BRING

**1.** A notebook and a pencil to write down or draw what you see.

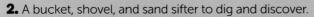

**2.** A bucket, shovel, and sand sifter to dig and discover.

**3.** Your curiosity, a grown-up to help you explore—**and this book!**

# Soft and Squishy Sand

When you walk on the beach, you may feel sand under your feet. Sand is made of rocks and shells that have been crushed into very small bits called grains.

Grains of sand can be smooth or rough, sticky or silky. Sandy beaches come in many different colors.

BLACK SAND BEACH, HAWAII, U.S.A.

ORANGE SAND BEACH, ITALY

PINK SAND BEACH, INDONESIA

WHITE SAND BEACH, AUSTRALIA

Rocky beaches can have huge stones or smaller rocks and pebbles. Some of these rocks might even hold a fossil. A fossil is part of a living thing that has been saved in rock. It can be from millions of years ago!

FOSSIL

ROCKY BEACHES

## SEA GLASS

Sea glass forms when pieces of broken glass get tumbled around by the sea for many years.

9

# Home Sweet Home

A beach can have different kinds of habitats. A habitat is a place to live, kind of like a neighborhood. Here are a few beach habitats and some of the plants and animals that live in them.

**TIDE POOLS.** A tide pool is a small or large puddle of seawater on a rocky beach. When the tide is high, open spaces in the rocks fill with water. When the tide rolls back out, water and a lot of creatures are left behind.

## LOW AND HIGH TIDE

Low tide is when the ocean's water moves far away from the shore. High tide is when the water comes up high onto the shore. Most shores have two low tides and two high tides every day.

LOW TIDE

HIGH TIDE

**DUNES.** A dune is a hill of sand. Dunes form in rows along the beach. Grasses and other plants can grow on dunes. Snakes, insects, birds, and small mammals make their homes here.

**SHORES.** The shore is where land meets water. Sand crabs dig here. Sea lions hang out on rocks. From the shore of a beach, you can see the water in front of you.

**IN THE WATER.** Shrimp scurry on the seafloor. Fish and turtles swim. Seaweed floats on the water. Dolphins leap above the waves. Splash!

Turn the page to **meet more beach creatures!**

# Crawling **Crabs**

Crabs dig in the sand and live in the sea. They have 10 legs. Two of their legs usually have claws on them. Crabs are crustaceans. Crustaceans are animals with a hard shell on the outside of their bodies.

**CAN YOU CRAWL LIKE A CRAB?**

**CHECK ME OUT!**

## ATLANTIC GHOST CRAB

**MY SIZE:** slightly smaller than the length of a crayon

**MY COLOR:** pale yellow to grayish white

**MY HOME:** the Atlantic coast of North and South America

**MY FOOD:** insects, crustaceans, clams, turtle eggs and hatchlings

THE GHOST CRAB SCARES OFF ENEMIES WITH A LOUD **"GROWL"** FROM **ITS STOMACH!**

# MEET MORE CRABS

### HERMIT CRAB
This tiny crab moves into an old snail shell to protect its soft body.

### HAIRY CRAB
This crab has one claw that's bigger than the other and hair on its shell and legs.

### SAND CRAB
At feeding time, sand crabs bury their back legs in the sand, face the sea, and eat plankton that floats to them.

### SAND BUBBLER CRAB
These crabs leave behind tiny balls of sand when they eat.

### SLIPPER LOBSTER
Slipper lobsters don't have claws! They have flat bodies that allow them to blend in with rocks on the ocean floor.

### BARNACLES
These tiny animals stick themselves to rocks, boats, and even other sea creatures.

# More Cool

### LOBSTER
Most lobsters are a dark brown color. But some rare ones are blue!

**SWARM OF KRILL**

**KRILL**

These small animals swim in giant swarms. This makes it easy for whales, fish, and seabirds to eat a lot of krill at once.

**WHALE**

**KRILL CLOSE-UP**

# CRUSTACEANS

**SHRIMP**

Shrimp have thin bodies, fan-shaped tails, long antennae, and a lot of legs.

**WHAT COULD YOU DO IF YOU HAD CLAWS INSTEAD OF HANDS?**

SOME BEACHES ARE **COVERED** IN SHELLS.

CONCH SHELL

**MY SIZE:** about as long as a notebook

**MY COLOR:** peach and pink

**MY HOME:** Caribbean Sea and nearby waters

# So Many **Shells**

Anybody home? Many beach creatures live inside shells. These shells come in different shapes, colors, and sizes. They can be big or small, smooth or bumpy.

A conch (pronounced KONK) is a large sea snail. Its eyes sit on long tubes called eyestalks. Can you see them?

QUEEN CONCH

## MORE SHELLS

What kinds of shells do you like to look for on the beach?

**COWRIE SHELL**

These shells are really shiny!

**JINGLE SHELL**

These thin, pearly shells are often used to make jewelry.

**TUSK SHELL**

These shells look like long, sharp teeth.

**CHAMBERED NAUTILUS**

This shell has many little "rooms" inside of it.

# A Shell Home

Shells are the hard outer skeleton of animals called mollusks. Mollusks have soft and squishy bodies. Their shells help protect them. When you find a shell at the beach, it is usually because a mollusk is not inside it anymore.

MUSSEL SHELL

A BIVALVE IS A MOLLUSK **WITH BOTH A TOP AND A BOTTOM SHELL.**

**CHECK ME OUT!** COQUINA CLAM

**MY SIZE:** smaller than the length of a paper clip

**MY COLOR:** white, yellow, pink, purple, or blue

**MY HOME:** along sandy beaches, worldwide

**MY FOOD:** plankton

# MEET MORE
# MOLLUSKS

TENTACLES

EYES

## SCALLOP

A scallop has a lot of eyes on the edge of its shell. It also has tentacles. These help the scallop sense danger.

## OYSTER

When bits of food get stuck inside an oyster shell, the animal wraps a lining around it. Over time, a pearl is formed.

A PEARL

## ABALONE
## (pronounced ABB-a-lo-nee)

This large sea snail has a strong foot that helps it hang on to rocks.

## MUSSEL

This bivalve uses threads that grow inside its shell to attach itself to rocks and other mussels.

GULLS FLY AROUND SAND DUNES, BUT THEY CAN ALSO BE **SPOTTED FAR FROM THE SEASHORE.**

**CHECK ME OUT!**

## RING-BILLED GULL

**MY SIZE:** about the length of a bowling pin

**MY COLOR:** white, gray, and black, with yellow beak and legs

**MY HOME:** North America

**MY FOOD:** almost everything

# Soaring Seabirds

Birds soar above the beach. They swoop down to the sea to catch fish. They caw, tweet, whistle, and sing! Some birds live at the beach year-round. Others just fly in for a visit at certain times.

Beaches are like playgrounds for birds! There is plenty of food to catch and lots of wind for gliding high in the sky.

RING-BILLED GULLS

### PUFFIN
A puffin can hold many fish in its mouth at once!

### PELICAN
The pelican dives from high in the air to scoop up fish in the sea.

### ARCTIC TERN
This bird flies thousands of miles every year—from the Arctic to the Antarctic.

**HOODED PLOVER**
This Australian bird lays spotted eggs on dunes.

# More Beach BIRDS

**REDDISH EGRET**
These birds walk in shallow salt water to catch fish.

## WHITE IBIS
This North American bird grabs insects and crabs to eat with its long, curved beak.

## BLUE-FOOTED BOOBY
These Central and South American birds dance and show off their colorful feet!

## NESTING BIRDS
Some birds dig holes in the sand to lay their eggs. Other birds use twigs to build nests on rocks. Seabird nests can be located on the shoreline, up on dunes, or in rocky areas.

BROWN BOOBY

## RAZORBILL
This black-and-white bird perches on rocky cliffs along the North Atlantic Ocean.

# Sea **Plants**

Many different kinds of plants grow in the sea. Algae, kelp, and seagrass feed some of the ocean's animals.

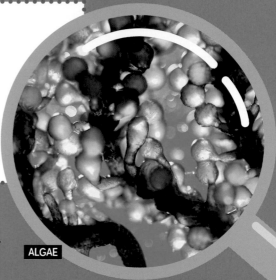

ALGAE

Most sea plants are a kind of algae. Some kinds of algae are so tiny you need a microscope to see them. Other kinds are as long as a basketball court!

MANGROVE FOREST

MANGROVES ARE A GROUP OF TREES AND SHRUBS THAT **USUALLY GROW IN SALT WATER.**

**KELP**

**MY SIZE:** from the length of a bed to the height of a 10-story building

**MY COLOR:** brown and green

**MY HOME:** in cold coastal waters of the Atlantic and Pacific Oceans

# SEAWEED

Seaweed comes in many different colors. It can be green, brown, red, gold, and even purple!

### SARGASSUM
This golden seaweed has little air-filled pouches that make it float.

### SEA GRAPES
This green algae looks like little grapes on a stem.

### SEAGRASS
This is the only flowering plant in the ocean.

# Beach Plants

Many plants grow in the sand on a beach. Grasses, shrubs, and flowers grow on dunes. They help hold these sandy hills in place.

**DUNE PLANTS ARE STRONG.** THEY GROW IN SALTY SAND AND CAN LIVE WITHOUT MUCH RAIN.

**CHECK ME OUT!**

## BEACH GRASS

**MY SIZE:** as tall as a baseball bat

**MY COLOR:** green

**MY HOME:** Atlantic Ocean coasts in parts of North America, Europe, Africa, and Asia

# MORE
# BEACH PLANTS

### RED SAND VERBENA
Small beach animals can hide under this plant's thick, green leaves.

### CREEPING BUTTERCUP
The yellow flowers of this plant attract insects.

### BEACH BUR
The leaves of this beach plant are a silvery green color.

# Tide Pool Life

A tide pool is always changing. It's not easy to live there. When the sea rushes in during high tide, large fish come looking for food. During low tide, animals can dry out. But tide pool creatures have ways to survive.

**CHECK ME OUT!** PURPLE SEA URCHIN

**MY SIZE:** about as long as a playing card

**MY COLOR:** purple

**MY HOME:** tide pools on the west coast of North America

**MY FOOD:** algae

A PURPLE SEA URCHIN **COVERS ITSELF** IN SHELLS, ROCKS, AND BITS OF ALGAE **TO HIDE DURING LOW TIDE.**

Tide pools are fun to explore! You can look for amazing animals and plants that live there. When you visit a tide pool, wear shoes that can grip slippery rocks. Explore tide pools when the water is calm, and find safe places to step.

ROCK POOLS, AUSTRALIA

## MEET MORE
# TIDE POOL ANIMALS

### ANEMONE
Anemones wave their tentacles in the water to catch food.

### LIMPET
This sea snail uses its shell to cut a space into a rock that it can squeeze into.

### SCULPIN
This little fish can survive out of water for a few hours during low tide.

### SKELETON SHRIMP
These tiny shrimp can be almost see-through. This helps them hide from hungry animals.

# Beach **Bugs**

Fleas, beetles, spiders, and worms hop, crawl, and dig at the beach. Most of them are tiny and the same color as the sand. But if you look carefully, you might be able to spot these creepy-crawlies.

THE SAND WOLF SPIDER **RUNS ACROSS THE SAND** TO CATCH BUGS TO EAT.

**CHECK ME OUT!** SAND WOLF SPIDER

**MY SIZE:** half the size of a paper clip

**MY COLOR:** whatever color the sand is

**MY HOME:** beaches of North and Central America

**MY FOOD:** insects

There is one GIANT beach bug that can be easy to spot: the horseshoe crab. Horseshoe crabs are not really crabs. They are related to spiders!

HORSESHOE CRAB

## MEET MORE BUGS

### HAIRY-NECKED TIGER BEETLE
This beetle digs holes in the sand to live in.

### SANDWORM
These worms leave behind squiggly piles of sand as they dig.

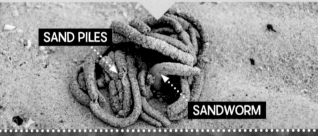

SAND PILES

SANDWORM

### BEACH HOPPER
These tiny crustaceans can jump high in the air!

A SEAHORSE MIGHT LOOK LIKE A HORSE, **BUT IT IS A FISH!**

FIN

**CHECK ME OUT!** SPINY SEAHORSE

**MY SIZE:** about the size of a dollar bill

**MY COLOR:** yellow, pink, or green

**MY HOME:** Indo-Pacific Ocean

**MY FOOD:** small crustaceans and fish larvae

# Fantastic Fish

Fish of all shapes and sizes swim in the ocean waters near the beach. But big or small, all fish have gills to breathe and fins to move through the water.

SEAHORSES **USE THEIR TAILS** TO HOLD ON TO SEAGRASS.

### RAY

This fish has fins that look like wings! It flaps these big fins to swim.

### SARDINES

These small, silvery fish swim in large groups called schools.

### FLOUNDER

These fish have flat bodies. They lie hidden in the sand on the seafloor to catch other fish.

### PIPEFISH

Can you spot this tiny pipefish swaying with the seagrass?

# Super Sea Stars

Most sea stars have five arms. But some kinds can grow as many as 40 arms! Sea stars have a superpower. They can grow back arms that have come off.

SEA STARS HAVE **SUCTION CUPS** ON THEIR ARMS.

**CHECK ME OUT!**

## SEA STAR

**MY SIZE:** about the length of two or three crayons, end to end

**MY COLOR:** so many different colors

**MY HOME:** every ocean in the world

**MY FOOD:** clams, oysters, and sea snails

# MORE COOL
## SEA CREATURES

### OCTOPUS

An octopus has eight arms attached to a soft, squishy body.

### SAND DOLLAR

This animal is covered in tiny spines that help it walk, hide, and eat.

### LEAFY SEA DRAGON

This fish has frilly fins that help it blend in with seaweed.

# Terrific Turtles

Sea turtles swim far out in the ocean and also close to shore. Mother sea turtles crawl onto the beach to lay their eggs in the sand. After the eggs hatch, the baby turtles crawl to the water.

## MEET MORE SEA TURTLES

### LEATHERBACK TURTLE
These are the largest sea turtles in the world!

### GREEN TURTLE
Once a year, female green turtles go back to the beach where they were born.

### HAWKSBILL TURTLE
These turtles feed on sea sponges and jellyfish close to shore.

THE LOGGERHEAD TURTLE HAS A LARGE HEAD WITH **STRONG JAWS.**

**CHECK ME OUT!** LOGGERHEAD TURTLE

**MY SIZE:** about as long as a seven-year-old child is tall

**MY COLOR:** reddish brown

**MY HOME:** warm waters worldwide

**MY FOOD:** clams and sea urchins

# Jiggly Jellyfish

These creatures twirl and float through the sea. Some jellyfish are colorful. Others are clear. This makes them hard to see in the water.

CRYSTAL JELLY ON THE SHORE

Jellyfish are also called jellies. Their bodies look like blobs. They have long tentacles that can sting. Jellyfish don't have brains, hearts, bones, or blood. They are made mostly of water.

NORTHERN SEA NETTLE

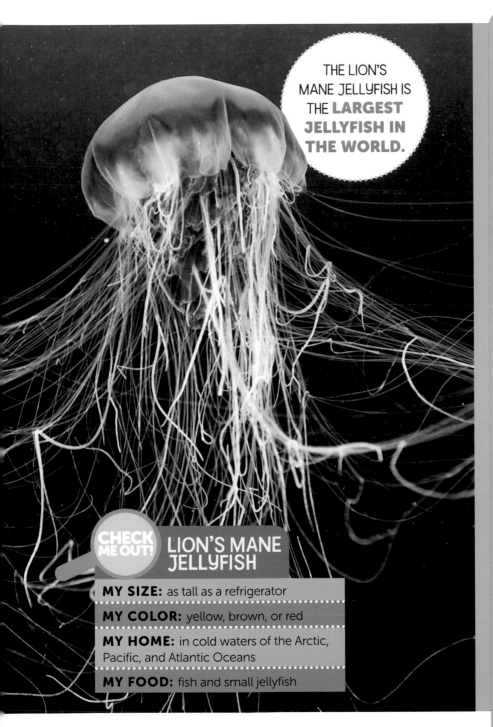

THE LION'S MANE JELLYFISH IS THE **LARGEST JELLYFISH IN THE WORLD.**

**CHECK ME OUT!** LION'S MANE JELLYFISH

**MY SIZE:** as tall as a refrigerator

**MY COLOR:** yellow, brown, or red

**MY HOME:** in cold waters of the Arctic, Pacific, and Atlantic Oceans

**MY FOOD:** fish and small jellyfish

# MEET MORE JELLIES

### MOON JELLY

This jellyfish is named for its body shape. It looks like the moon.

### MEDITERRANEAN JELLYFISH

It's also known as the "fried egg" jellyfish. Can you see why?

### PURPLE-STRIPED JELLYFISH

This jelly has 16 purple stripes.

39

# Marvelous
# Marine Mammals

Mammals are animals that drink their mother's milk and breathe air. Mammals that live in the ocean, like the manatee, are called marine mammals. Manatees usually live close to shore.

CHECK ME OUT! **WEST INDIAN MANATEE**

**MY SIZE:** about the length of a car

**MY COLOR:** gray

**MY HOME:** in warm waters along the eastern coasts of North, Central, and South America

**MY FOOD:** sea plants

MANATEES CAN STAY **UNDERWATER FOR UP TO 20 MINUTES** AT A TIME.

# MEET MORE
# MARINE MAMMALS

### HUMPBACK WHALE

This large whale can leap out of the water. This movement is called breaching.

### SEA OTTER

Otters use rocks as tools to help them open shells and eat the animals inside.

### WALRUS

Walruses have long teeth called tusks. They live in cold, Arctic seas.

### BOTTLENOSE DOLPHIN

These animals can live in shallow water close to shore or in deep ocean water. It's fun to watch them leap!

CALIFORNIA SEA LION

# Sea Lion or Seal?

Sea lions and seals look a lot alike. They both have long bodies, flippers, and whiskers. And they both mostly live close to shore.

HARBOR SEAL

Here's how to spot the difference between sea lions and seals:

BOTH SEA LIONS AND SEALS ARE **SUPER SEA DIVERS!**

| SEA LIONS | VS. | SEALS |
|---|---|---|
| | **EARS & VOICE** Sea lions have ear flaps and bark noisily. Seals don't have ear flaps, only holes. They don't make much noise. | |
| | **MOVEMENT** Sea lions walk on their flippers. Seals wiggle on their bellies. | |
| | **BEHAVIOR** Sea lions gather in large groups on the shore. Seals spend more time alone, in the sea. | |
| | **FOOD** Sea lions eat fish, squid, and octopuses. Seals eat mainly fish. | |

# BEACH SOUNDS

## Copy the sounds of the beach! Can you ...

MAKE BUBBLES LIKE A FISH?

WHISTLE LIKE THE WIND?

SQUAWK LIKE A SEAGULL?

BARK LIKE A WALRUS?

SWOOSH LIKE THE WAVES?

CLACK LIKE A CRAB?

# BEACH DAY AT HOME

If you can't go to the beach, bring the beach to you! Dress in your swimsuit and put on goggles or sunglasses. Spread out towels on the floor and ask a grown-up to help you play a recording of some beach sounds. Draw and cut out pictures of shells and sea creatures for some beachy decorations. Read this book aloud and dream of your perfect beach day!

# GLOSSARY

**ALGAE** living things that usually grow in water, such as kelp and other seaweed

**ANEMONE** a sea animal with tentacles around its mouth

**BREACHING** when a whale leaps above the water

**COAST** the land near a seashore

**CRUSTACEAN** an animal that has a shell on the outside of its body

**DUNE** a large hill of sand on a beach

**FOSSIL** the preserved remains of a living thing from millions of years ago

**GILLS** organs that fish use to breathe in the water

**HABITAT** the place where an animal or plant lives

**LARVAE** fish eggs that have just hatched

**MICROSCOPE** a scientific instrument that makes small objects look larger

**MOLLUSK** a soft-bodied animal that usually has a hard shell

**PLANKTON** very tiny plants and animals that float in the sea

**SHORE** where the land meets a large body of water

**SKELETON** the bones inside the bodies of some animals, such as mammals, fish, and birds

**SPINES** tiny, hairlike "feet" that cover a sand dollar's body

**TIDE** the rising and falling of the ocean's water

# INDEX

# Photo
# Credits

AL = Alamy Stock Photo; AS = Adobe Stock; GI = Getty Images; SS = Shutterstock; Cover (scallop shell), Aleksandr Simonov/AS; (sea star), Dariusz Jarzabek/AS; (sea horse), Rich Carey/SS; (sea turtle), David Carbo/SS; (fish), chonlasub woravichan/SS; (hermit crab), Liumangtiger/Dreamstime; Spine (sea star), Dariusz Jarzabek/AS; Back cover (scallop shell), Alexander Raths/SS; (jellyfish), bridgendboy/AS; (sea urchin), NatalieJean/SS; 1, shanemyersphoto/AS; 2 UP, FPLV/AS; 2 LO, Pavel Timofeev/AS; 3 UP LE, John Warburton-Lee Photography/AL; 3 UP CTR, damedias/AS; 3 UP RT, Federica Grassi/GI; 3 LO, Nature Picture Library/AL; 4 (shells), Jenifoto/AS; 4, lucky-photo/AS; 5 UP LE, masar1920/AS; 5 UP RT, Eric Isselée/AS; 5 CTR LE, Harry Collins/AS; 5 CTR RT, Kevin/AS; 5 LO LE, Gamut Stock Images Pvt Ltd/AL; 5 LO RT, Dariusz Jarzabek/AS; 6 UP, JonikFoto/AS; 6 CTR LE, koosen/SS; 6 CTR RT, AlexRoz/SS; 6 LO, Soloviova Liudmyla/AS; 7 UP LE, Waldemarus/SS; 7 UP RT, Serhii Tsyhanok/SS; 7 LO LE, agefotostock/AL; 7 CTR RT, Jessica Peterson/GI; 7 LO, Bell nipon/SS; 8 UP, Africa Studio/SS; 8 CTR LE, Photo Image/SS; 8 CTR RT, Gabriele Maltinti/AS; 8 LO LE, wanderskyy/SS; 8 LO RT, nelzajamal/AS; 9 UP LE, Derek Victor/AS; 9 UP RT, Milan Gonda/AL; 9 CTR, Aleksandr Volkov/AS; 9 LO LE, onstantin_Khilko/SS; 9 LO RT, Daguimagery/AS; 10 (yellow tang fish), Eric Isselée/AS; 10 (jewelfish), Grigorev Mikhail/SS; 10 (blue tang fish), jeby69/GI; 10 CTR, David Hall/Minden Pictures; 10 LO BOTH, Michael Marten; 11 (powder blue tang fish), chonlasub woravichan/SS; 11 UP LE, Gloria Moeller/AS; 11 UP RT, creativenature/AS; 11 LO LE, andrewburgess/AS; 11 LO RT, damedias/AS ; 12, Kevin Oke Photograph/AS; 13 UP LE, Subphoto/AS; 13 UP RT, Eric Isselée/SS; 13 LO LE, blickwinkel/AL; 13 LO CTR, Vinicius-Moreira/GI; 13 LO RT, evannovostro/AS; 14 UP LE, MrPreecha/AS; 14 UP RT, Theo AlLOfs/Minden Pictures; 14 LO, Sue Daly/Minden Pictures; 14 LO LE, Richard Herrmann/Minden Pictures; 15 UP RT, Education Images/GI; 15 LO, kerkla/GI; 16 INSET, Oleksandrum/AS; 16, serge114/AS; 17 UP LE, Jenifoto/AS; 17 LO LE, Stephen Frink/Digital Vision; 17 (cowrie), vartzbed/AS; 17 (jingle), Jerrry G/AS; 17 (tusk), Dave Marsden/AL; 17 (nautilus), emotionpicture/AS; 18 UP, oxxyzay/AS; 18 LO, tbkmedia.de/AL; 19 UP LE, Alex Mustard/Minden Pictures; 19 UP RT, Aleksandr Simonov/AS; 19 CTR LE, photoDISC; 19 CTR, Sergio Hanquet/Minden Pictures; 19 CTR RT, Clay Bolt/Minden Pictures; 19 LO LE, Picture Partners/AS; 19 LO CTR, Freer/AS; 19 LO RT, DoublePHOTO studio/SS; 20, Ludwig/AS; 21 LE, Brian Lasenby/SS; 21 UP RT, creativenature.nl/AS; 21 CTR RT, Arthur Morris/GI; 21 LO RT, DieterMeyrl/GI; 22 UP LE, Imogen Warren/SS; 22 UP RT, Phil Lowe/AS; 22 LO LE, All Canada Photos/AL; 22 LO RT, BIOSPHOTO/AL; 23 LE, BruceCampos/GI; 23 RT, Juergen Freund/AL; 24 UP, chokniti/AS; 24 LO, Chad Zuber/SS; 25 UP, Brent Durand/GI; 25 LO LE, Mark Conlin/AL; 25 LO CTR, damedias/AS; 25 LO RT, Shane Gross/Nature Picture Library; 26, Henrik Larsson/AS; 27 UP LE, Universal Images GroUP North America LLC / DeAgostini/AL; 27 UP RT, Natural History Collection/AL; 27 LO LE, Carl Morrow/AS; 27 LO RT, Derrick Ditchburn/Science Source; 28 UP, Georgette Douwma/Minden Pictures; 28 LO, PJsandsmark/AS; 29 UP, Ryan Newton/GI; 29 CTR, randimal/AS; 29 LO LE, Andrew J. Martinez/Science Source; 29 LO CTR, jonathan nguyen/AL; 29 LO RT, Brent Durand/GI; 30, Ed Reschke/GI; 31 UP, Mira/AL; 31 LO LE, SDym Photography/AL; 31 CTR RT, anton eine/EyeEm/AS ; 31 LO RT, Alan Gregg/AL; 32, Alex Mustard/Nature Picture Library; 33 LE, Shane Gross/Nature Picture Library; 33 (ray), Shane Gross/Minden Pictures; 33 (sardines), sLOwmotiongli/GI; 33 (flounder), Drew McArthur/SS; 33 (pipefish), Michael Patrick O'Neill/AL; 34 UP, All Canada Photos/AL; 34 INSET, Sue Daly/Nature Picture Library; 35 LE, Alex Mustard/Nature Picture Library; 35 UP RT, Olga Visavi/SS; 35 LO RT, Fred Bavendam/Minden Pictures; 36 UP, Shane Gross/SS; 36 LO LE, Doug Perrine/Minden Pictures; 36 LO CTR, Nattawud Groodngoen/SS; 36 LO RT, whitcomberd/AS; 36-37, Charlie Reaney/SS; 38 UP LE, Jirik V/SS; 38 UP RT, Joe McBride-Crisp/SS; 38 LO, Bidouze Stephane/Dreamstime; 39 LE, Cultura RM Exclusive/Alexander Semenov/GI; 39 UP RT, damedias/AS; 39 CTR RT, Mark Barrett/AS; 39 LO RT, Lukas Gojda/SS; 40, Thierry Eidenweil/SS; 41 UP, Martin Prochazkacz/SS; 41 LO LE, Jody/AS; 41 LO CTR, zanskar/GI; 41 RT, Shawn Jackson/Dreamstime; 42 UP, leonardogonzalez/AS; 42 LO, Nature Picture Library/AL; 43 (sea lion ears), Tim Fitzharris/Minden Pictures; 43 (seal ears), KGrif/GI; 43 (sea lion movement), Hedrus/AS; 43 (seal movement), Dirk/AS; 43 (sea lion behavior), Stephanie/AS; 43 (seal behavior), George Karbus Photography/GI; 43 (squid), Chris/AS; 43 (fish), Four Oaks/AS; 44 UP LE, Peter Cade/GI; 44 UP CTR, Jillian Cain/AS; 44 UP RT, Lux Ferro/AS; 44 LO LE, Michael S. Nolan/AL; 44 LO CTR, helivideo/AS; 44 LO RT, Steve BLOom Images/AL; 45 UP LE, Peteri/SS; 45 UP RT, Serhii Tsyhanok/SS; 45 CTR LE, Kletr/SS; 45 LO, Westend61/GI; 46 UP, Fatih/AS; 46 LO LE, Eric Isselée/AS; 46 LO CTR, jeby69/GI; 46 LO RT, Shane Gross/SS; 47 UP, Tamela/AS; 47 LO, Aleksandr Simonov/AS

To the Long Beach High School (NY) Class of '98 —A.B.

Published by National Geographic Partners, LLC, Washington, DC 20036.

Designed by Sanjida Rashid

The publisher gratefully acknowledges Dr. Shayle Benjamin Matsuda, conservation research scientist at Shedd Aquarium, and Dr. David Gruber, National Geographic Explorer and distinguished professor of biology at City University of New York, for their expert review of this book. Many thanks also to Dr. Tovah P. Klein, director of the Barnard College Center for Toddler Development, for her advice and expertise, as well as project manager Grace Hill Smith, editorial assistant Emily Fego, photo editors Nicole DiMella and Lori Epstein, and researcher Alicia Klepeis.

**Library of Congress Cataloging-in-Publication Data**

Names: Brydon, Alli, author.

Title: Explore the beach / Alli Brydon.

Other titles: Little kids first nature guide explore the beach

Description: Washington, D.C. : National Geographic Kids, [2023] I Series: Little kids first nature guide I Includes index. I Audience: Ages 4-8 I Audience: Grades K-1 I

Identifiers: LCCN 2022023697 I ISBN 9781426373688 (paperback) I ISBN 9781426375064 (library binding)

Subjects: LCSH: Seashore ecology--Juvenile literature. I Seashore animals--Juvenile literature. I Seashore Plants--Juvenile literature.

Classification: LCC QH541.5.S35 B79 2023 I DDC 577.69/9--dc23/eng/20220707

LC record available at https://lccn.loc.gov/2022023697

Printed in China

23/RRDH/1